Congress. Senate United States.

Standing Rules for Conducting Business in the Senate of the

United States

Congress. Senate United States.

Standing Rules for Conducting Business in the Senate of the United States

ISBN/EAN: 9783337155810

Printed in Europe, USA, Canada, Australia, Japan

Cover: Foto ©ninafisch / pixelio.de

More available books at **www.hansebooks.com**

IN THE SENATE OF THE UNITED STATES.

STANDING RULES

FOR

CONDUCTING BUSINESS

IN THE

SENATE OF THE UNITED STATES

REPORTED BY

THE COMMITTEE ON RULES.

JANUARY 11. 1884.—Adopted by the Senate. and to go into
effect January 21, 1884.

WASHINGTON:
GOVERNMENT PRINTING OFFICE.
1884.

STANDING RULES

FOR

CONDUCTING BUSINESS IN THE SENATE OF THE UNITED STATES.

RULES.

DAILY SESSIONS.

RULE I.

APPOINTMENT OF A SENATOR TO THE CHAIR.

1. In the absence of the Vice-President, the Senate shall choose a President *pro tempore*.

2. In the absence of the Vice-President, and pending the election of a President *pro tempore*, the Secretary of the Senate, or in his absence the Chief Clerk, shall perform the duties of the Chair.

3. The President *pro tempore* shall have the right to name in open Senate, or, if absent, in writing, a Senator to perform the duties of the Chair; but such substitution shall not extend beyond an adjournment, except by unanimous consent.

RULE II.

OATHS, ETC.

The oaths or affirmations required by the Constitution and prescribed by law shall be taken and subscribed by each Senator, in open Senate, before entering upon his duties.

RULE III.

COMMENCEMENT OF DAILY SESSIONS.

1. The Presiding Officer having taken the chair, and a quorum being present, the Journal of the preceding day shall be read, and any mistake made in the entries corrected. The reading of the Journal shall not be suspended unless by unanimous consent; and when any motion shall be made to amend or correct the same, it shall be deemed a privileged question, and proceeded with until disposed of.

2. A quorum shall consist of a majority of the Senators duly chosen and sworn.

RULE IV.

JOURNAL.

1. The proceedings of the Senate shall be briefly and accurately stated on the Journal. Messages of the President in full; titles of bills and joint resolutions, and such parts as shall be affected by proposed amendments; every vote, and a brief statement of the contents of each petition, memorial, or paper presented to the Senate, shall be entered.

2. The legislative, the executive, the confidential legislative proceedings, and the proceedings when sitting as a Court of Impeachment, shall each be recorded in a separate book.

RULE V.

QUORUM—ABSENT SENATORS MAY BE SENT FOR.

1. No Senator shall absent himself from the service of the Senate without leave.

2. If, at any time during the daily sessions of the Senate, a question shall be raised by any Senator as to the presence of a quorum, the Presiding Officer shall forthwith direct the Secretary to call the roll and shall announce the result, and these proceedings shall be without debate.

3. Whenever upon such roll-call it shall be ascertained that a quorum is not present, a majority of the Senators present may direct the Sergeant-at-Arms to request, and, when necessary, to compel the attendance of the absent Senators, which order shall be determined without debate; and pending its execution, and until a quorum shall be present, no debate nor motion, except to adjourn, shall be in order.

RULE VI.

PRESENTATION OF CREDENTIALS.

1. The presentation of the credentials of Senators elect and other questions of privilege shall always be in order, except during the reading and correction of the Journal, while a question of order or a motion to adjourn is pending, or while the Senate is dividing; and all questions and motions arising or made upon the presentation of such credentials shall be proceeded with until disposed of.

2. The Secretary shall keep a record of the certificates of election of Senators by entering in a well-bound book kept for that purpose the date of the election, the name of the person elected and the vote given at the election, the date of the certificate, the name of the governor and the secretary of state signing and countersigning the same, and the State from which such Senator is elected.

RULE VII.

MORNING BUSINESS.

1. After the Journal is read, the Presiding Officer shall lay before the Senate, messages from the President, reports and communications from the heads of Departments, and other communications addressed to the Senate; and such bills, joint resolutions, and other messages from the House of Representatives as may remain upon his table from any previous day's session undisposed of. The Presiding Officer shall then call for, in the following order:

"The presentation of petitions and memorials;

" Reports of Standing and Select Committees;

" The introduction of bills and joint resolutions;

" Concurrent and other resolutions; "

all which shall be received and disposed of in such order unless unanimous consent shall be otherwise given.

2. Until the morning business shall have been concluded, and so announced from the chair, or until the hour of one o'clock has arrived, no motion to proceed to the consideration of any bill, resolution, report of a committee, or other subject upon the Calendar shall be entertained by the Presiding Officer, unless by unanimous consent; and if such consent be given the

motion shall not be subject to amendment, and shall be decided without debate upon the merits of the subject proposed to be taken up.

3. Every petition or memorial shall be referred, without putting the question, unless objection to such reference is made; in which case all motions for the reception or reference of such petition. memorial. or other paper shall be put in the order in which the same shall be made, and shall not be open to amendment, except to add instructions.

4. Before any petition or memorial shall be received, it shall be signed by the petitioner or memorialist, and a brief statement of its contents made by the Presiding Officer or Senator presenting it. But no petition or memorial or other paper signed by citizens or subjects of a foreign power shall be received. unless the same be transmitted to the Senate by the President.

RULE VIII.

ORDER OF BUSINESS.

At the conclusion of the morning business for each day, unless upon motion the Senate shall at any time otherwise order, the Senate will proceed to the consideration of the Calendar of bills and resolutions. and continue such consideration until 2 o'clock; and bills and resolutions that are not objected to shall be taken up in their order. and each Senator shall be entitled to speak once and for five minutes only upon any question; and the objection may be interposed at any stage of the proceedings, but upon motion the Senate may continue such consideration; and this order shall commence immediately after the call for "concurrent and other resolutions," and shall take precedence of the unfinished business and other special orders. But if the Senate shall proceed with the consideration of any matter notwithstanding an objection, the foregoing provisions touching debate shall not apply.

RULE IX.

ORDER OF BUSINESS—Continued.

Immediately after the consideration of cases not objected to upon the Calendar is completed, and not later than two o'clock, if there shall be no special orders for that time, the Calendar of General Orders shall be taken up and proceeded with in its

order, beginning with the first subject on the Calendar next after the last subject disposed of in proceeding with the Calendar; and in such case the following motions shall be in order at any time as priviluged motions, save as against a motion to adjourn, or to proceed to the consideration of Executive business, or questions of privilege, to wit:

First. A motion to proceed to the consideration of an appropriation or revenue bill.

Second. A motion to proceed to the consideration of any other bill on the Calendar, which motion shall not be open to amendment.

Third. A motion to pass over the pending subject, which, if carried, shall have the effect to leave such subject without prejudice in its place on the Calendar.

Fourth. A motion to place such subject at the foot of the Calendar.

Each of the foregoing motions shall be decided without debate, and shall have precedence in the order above named, and may be submitted as in the nature and with all the rights of questions of order.

RULE X.

SPECIAL ORDERS.

1. Any subject may, by a vote of two-thirds of the Senators present, be made a special order; and when the time so fixed for its consideration arrives, the Presiding Officer shall lay it before the Senate unless there be unfinished business of the preceding day; and if it is not finally disposed of on that day, it shall take its place on the Calendar of Special Orders, in the order of time at which it was made special, unless it shall become by adjournment the unfinished business.

2. When two or more special orders have been made for the same time they shall have precedence according to the order in which they were severally assigned, and that order shall only be changed by direction of the Senate.

RULE XI.

OBJECTION TO READING A PAPER.

When the reading of a paper is called for, and objected to, it shall be determined by a vote of the Senate, without debate.

RULE XII.

VOTING, ETC.

1, When the yeas and nays are ordered, the names of Senators shall be called alphabetically; and each Senator shall, without debate, declare his assent or dissent to the question, unless excused by the Senate; and no Senator shall be permitted to vote after the decision shall have been announced by the Presiding Officer, but may for sufficient reasons, with unanimous consent, change or withdraw his vote. No motion to suspend this rule shall be in order, nor shall the Presiding Officer entertain any request to suspend it by unanimous consent.

2. When a Senator declines to vote on call of his name, he shall be required to assign his reasons therefor, and having assigned them, the Presiding Officer shall submit the question to the Senate: "Shall the Senator, for the reasons assigned by him, be excused from voting?" which shall be decided without debate; and these proceedings shall be had after the roll-call and before the result is announced; and any further proceedings in reference thereto shall be after such announcement.

RULE XIII.

RECONSIDERATION.

1. When a question has been decided by the Senate, any Senator voting with the prevailing side may, on the same day or on either of the next two days of actual session thereafter, move a reconsideration; and if the Senate shall refuse to reconsider, or upon reconsideration shall affirm its first decision, no further motion to reconsider shall be in order unless by unanimous consent. Every motion to reconsider shall be decided by a majority vote, without debate, and may be laid on the table without affecting the question in reference to which the same is made, which shall be a final disposition of the motion.

2. When a bill, resolution, report, amendment, order, or message, upon which a vote has been taken, shall have gone out of the possession of the Senate, and been communicated to the House of Representatives, the motion to reconsider shall be accompanied by a motion to request the House to return the same; which last motion shall be acted upon immediately, and without debate, and if determined in the negative, shall be a final disposition of the motion to reconsider.

RULE XIV.

BILLS, JOINT RESOLUTIONS, AND RESOLUTIONS.

1. Whenever a bill or joint resolution shall be offered, its introduction shall, if objected to, be postponed for one day.

2. Every bill and joint resolution shall receive three readings previous to its passage; which readings shall be on three different days, unless the Senate unanimously direct otherwise; and the Presiding Officer shall give notice at each reading whether it be the first, second, or third.

3. No bill or joint resolution shall be committed or amended until it shall have been twice read, after which it may be referred to a committee; bills and joint resolutions introduced on leave, and bills and joint resolutions from the House of Representatives, shall be read once, and may be read twice, on the same day, if not objected to, for reference, but shall not be considered on that day as in Committee of the Whole, nor debated, except for reference, unless by unanimous consent.

4. Every bill and joint resolution reported from a committee, not having previously been read, shall be read once, and twice, if not objected to, on the same day, and placed on the Calendar in the order in which the same may be reported; and every bill and joint resolution introduced on leave, and every bill and joint resolution of the House of Representatives which shall have received a first and second reading without being referred to a committee, shall, if objection be made to further proceeding thereon, be placed on the Calendar.

5. All resolutions shall lie over one day for consideration unless by unanimous consent the Senate shall otherwise direct.

RULE XV.

BILLS—COMMITTEE OF THE WHOLE.

1. All bills and joint resolutions which shall have received two readings shall first be considered by the Senate as in Committee of the Whole, after which they shall be reported to the Senate; and any amendments made in Committee of the Whole shall again be considered by the Senate, after which further amendments may be proposed.

2. When a bill or resolution shall have been ordered to be read a third time, it shall not be in order to propose amendments, unless by unanimous consent, but it shall be in order at any time before the passage of any bill or resolution, to move

its commitment; and when the bill or resolution shall again be reported from the committee, it shall be placed on the Calendar, and when again considered by the Senate, it shall be as in Committee of the Whole.

6. Whenever a private bill is under consideration, it shall be in order to move, as a substitute for it, a resolution of the Senate referring the case to the Court of Claims, under the provisions of the act approved March 3, 1883.

RULE XVI.

AMENDMENTS TO APPROPRIATION BILLS.

1. All general appropriation bills shall be referred to the Committee on Appropriations, except bills making appropriations for rivers and harbors, which shall be referred to the Committee on Commerce; and no amendments shall be received to any general appropriation bill, the effect of which will be to increase an appropriation already contained in the bill, or to add a new item of appropriation, unless it be made to carry out the provisions of some existing law, or treaty stipulation, or act, or resolution previously passed by the Senate during that session; or unless the same be moved by direction of a standing or select committee of the Senate, or proposed in pursuance of an estimate of the head of some one of the Departments.

2. All amendments to general appropriation bills moved by direction of a standing or select committee of the Senate, proposing to increase an appropriation already contained in the bill, or to add new items of appropriation, shall, at least one day before they are considered, be referred to the Committee on Appropriations, and when actually proposed to the bill, no amendment proposing to increase the amount stated in such amendment shall be received; in like manner amendments proposing new items of appropriation to river and harbor bills shall, before being considered, be referred to the Committee on Commerce; also amendments to bills establishing post-roads, proposing new post-roads, shall, before being considered, be referred to the Committee on Post-Offices and Post-Roads.

3. No amendment which proposes general legislation shall be received to any general appropriation bill, nor shall any amendment not germane or relevant to the subject-matter contained in the bill be received; nor shall any amendment to any item or clause of such bill be received which does not directly

relate thereto; and all questions of relevancy of amendments under this rule, when raised, shall be submitted to the Senate and be decided without debate; and any amendment to a general appropriation bill may be laid on the table without prejudice to the bill.

4. No amendment, the object of which is to provide for a private claim, shall be received to any general appropriation bill, unless it be to carry out the provisions of an existing law or a treaty stipulation, which shall be cited on the face of the amendment.

RULE XVII.

AMENDMENT MAY BE LAID ON THE TABLE WITHOUT PREJUDICE TO THE BILL.

When an amendment proposed to any pending measure is laid on the table it shall not carry with it, or prejudice, such measure.

RULE XVIII.

AMENDMENTS—DIVISION OF A QUESTION.

If the question in debate contains several propositions, any Senator may have the same divided, except a motion to strike out and insert, which shall not be divided; but the rejection of a motion to strike out and insert one proposition shall not prevent a motion to strike out and insert a different proposition; nor shall it prevent a motion simply to strike out; nor shall the rejection of a motion to strike out prevent a motion to strike out and insert. But pending a motion to strike out and insert, the part to be stricken out and the part to be inserted shall each be regarded for the purpose of amendment as a question; and motions to amend the part to be stricken out shall have precedence.

RULE XIX.

DEBATE.

1. When a Senator desires to speak he shall rise and address the Presiding Officer, and shall not proceed until he is recognized, and the Presiding Officer shall recognize the Senator who shall first address him. No Senator shall interrupt another Senator in debate without his consent, and to obtain such consent he shall first address the Presiding Officer; and no Senator shall speak more than twice upon any one question in debate

on the same day without leave of the Senate; which shall be determined without debate.

2. If any Senator, in speaking or otherwise, transgress the rules of the Senate, the Presiding Officer shall, or any Senator may, call him to order; and when a Senator shall be called to order he shall sit down, and not proceed without leave of the Senate, which, if granted, shall be upon motion that he be allowed to proceed in order; which motion shall be determined without debate.

3. If a Senator be called to order for words spoken in debate, upon the demand of the Senator or of any other Senator the exceptionable words shall be taken down in writing, and read at the table for the information of the Senate.　．

RULE XX.

QUESTIONS OF ORDER.

1. A question of order may be raised at any stage of the proceedings, except when the Senate is dividing, and, unless submitted to the Senate, shall be decided by the Presiding Officer without debate, subject to an appeal to the Senate; when an appeal is taken any subsequent question of order, which may arise before the decision of such appeal, shall be decided by the Presiding Officer without debate; and every appeal therefrom shall be decided at once, and without debate; and any appeal may be laid on the table without prejudice to the pending proposition, and thereupon shall be held as affirming the decision of the Presiding Officer.

2. The Presiding Officer may submit any question of order for the decision of the Senate.

RULE XXI.

MOTIONS.

1 All motions shall be reduced to writing, if desired by the Presiding Officer or by any Senator, and shall be read before the same shall be debated.

2. Any motion or resolution may be withdrawn or modified by the mover at any time before a decision, amendment, or ordering of the yeas and nays, except a motion to reconsider, which shall not be withdrawn without leave.

STANDING RULES OF THE SENATE. 13

RULE XXII.

PRECEDENCE OF MOTIONS.

When a question is pending no motion shall be received
but—
To adjourn,
To adjourn to a day certain, or that when the Senate adjourn,
it shall be to a day certain,
To take a recess,
To proceed to the consideration of executive business,
To lay on the table,
To postpone indefinitely,
To postpone to a day certain,
To commit,
To amend;
which several motions shall have precedence as they stand ar-
ranged; and the motions relating to adjournment, to take a
recess, to proceed to the consideration of executive business,
to lay on the table, shall be decided without debate.

RULE XXIII.

PREAMBLES.

When a bill or resolution is accompanied by a preamble, the
question shall first be put on the bill or resolution and then on
the preamble, which may be withdrawn by a mover before an
amendment of the same, or ordering of the yeas and nays; or
it may be laid on the table without prejudice to the bill or resolution, and shall be a final disposition of such preamble.

RULE XXIV.

APPOINTMENT OF COMMITTEES.

1. In the appointment of the standing committees, the Senate, unless otherwise ordered, shall proceed by ballot to appoint
severally the chairman of each committee, and then, by one
ballot, the other members necessary to complete the same. A
majority of the whole number of votes given shall be necessary
to the choice of a chairman of a standing committee, but a plurality of votes shall elect the other members thereof. All other
committees shall be appointed by ballot, unless otherwise
ordered, and a plurality of votes shall appoint.

2. When a chairman of a committee shall resign or cease to serve on a committee. and the Presiding Officer be authorized by the Senate to fill the vacancy in such committee. unless specially otherwise ordered. it shall be only to fill up the number on the committee.

RULE XXV.

STANDING COMMITTEES.

1. The following standing committees shall be appointed at the commencement of each Congress. with leave to report by bill or otherwise:

A Committee on Agriculture and Forestry. to consist of nine Senators.

A Committee on Appropriations. to consist of nine Senators.

A Committee to Audit and Control the Contingent Expenses of the Senate. to consist of three Senators. to which shall be referred all resolutions directing the payment of money out of the contingent fund of the Senate. or creating a charge upon the same.

A Committee on Civil Service and Retrenchment. to consist of nine Senators.

A Committee on Claims. to consist of nine Senators.

A Committee on Commerce. to consist of eleven Senators.

A Committee on the District of Columbia. to consist of nine Senators.

A Committee on Education and Labor. to consist of nine Senators.

A Committee on Engrossed Bills. to consist of three Senators. which shall examine all bills. amendments. and joint resolutions before they go out of the possession of the Senate.

A Committee on Enrolled Bills. to consist of three Senators. which shall have power to act jointly with the same committee of the House of Representatives. and which. or some one of which. shall examine all bills or joint resolutions which shall have passed both Houses. to see that the same are correctly enrolled. and. when signed by the Speaker of the House and President of the Senate. shall forthwith present the same, when they shall have originated in the Senate, to the President of the United States in person. and report the fact and date of such presentation to the Senate.

A Committee on Epidemic Diseases. to consist of seven Senators.

A Committee to Examine the Several Branches of the Civil Service. to consist of five Senators.

A Committee on Expenditures of Public Money, to consist of seven Senators, which shall consider such measures tending to economy in public expenditures as shall be referred to it, and conduct all investigations into the expenditure of public money which shall be ordered by the Senate, unless the Senate shall otherwise direct.

A Committee on Finance, to consist of eleven Senators.

A Committee on Fisheries, to consist of seven Senators, to which shall be referred all matters relating to fish and fisheries.

A Committee on Foreign Relations, to consist of nine Senators.

A Committee on the Improvement of the Mississippi River, to consist of seven Senators.

A Committee on Indian Affairs, to consist of nine Senators.

A Committee on the Judiciary, to consist of nine Senators.

A Committee on the Library, to consist of three Senators, which shall have power to act jointly with the same committee of the House of Representatives.

A Committee on Manufactures, to consist of seven Senators.

A Committee on Military Affairs, to consist of nine Senators.

A Committee on Mines and Mining, to consist of seven Senators.

A Committee on Naval Affairs, to consist of nine Senators.

A Committee on Patents, to consist of seven Senators.

A Committee on Pensions, to consist of nine Senators.

A Committee on Post-Offices and Post-Roads, to consist of nine Senators.

A Committee on Printing, to consist of three Senators, which shall have power to act jointly with the same committee of the House of Representatives.

A Committee on Private Land Claims, to consist of five Senators.

A Committee on Privileges and Elections, to consist of nine Senators.

A Committee on Public Buildings and Grounds, to consist of five Senators, which shall have power to act jointly with the same committee of the House of Representatives.

A Committee on Public Lands, to consist of nine Senators.

A Committee on Railroads, to consist of eleven Senators.

A Committee on the Revision of the Laws of the United States, to consist of five Senators.

A Committee on Revolutionary Claims, to consist of five Senators.

A Committee on Rules, to consist of five Senators.

A Committee on Territories, to consist of nine Senators.

A Committee on Transportation Routes to the Seaboard, to consist of seven Senators.

2. The Committees to Audit and Control the Contingent Expenses of the Senate, on Printing, and on the Library shall continue and have power to act until their successors are appointed.

RULE XXVI.

REFERENCE TO COMMITTEES; MOTIONS TO DISCHARGE, AND REPORTS OF COMMITTEES TO LIE OVER.

1. When motions are made for reference of a subject to a select committee, or to a standing committee, the question of reference to a standing committee shall be put first; and a motion simply to refer shall not be open to amendment, except to add instructions.

2. All reports of committees and motions to discharge a committee from the consideration of a subject, and all subjects from which a committee shall be discharged, shall lie over one day for consideration, unless by unanimous consent the Senate shall otherwise direct.

RULE XXVII.

REPORTS OF CONFERENCE COMMITTEES.

The presentation of reports of committees of conference shall always be in order, except when the Journal is being read or a question of order or a motion to adjourn is pending, or while the Senate is dividing; and when received, the question of proceeding to the consideration of the report, if raised, shall be immediately put, and shall be determined without debate.

RULE XXVIII.

MESSAGES.

1. Messages from the President of the United States or from the House of Representatives may be received at any stage of proceedings, except while the Senate is dividing, or while the Journal is being read, or while a question of order or a motion to adjourn is pending.

2. Messages shall be sent to the House of Representatives by the Secretary, who shall previously certify the determination of the Senate upon all bills, joint resolutions, and other resolutions which may be communicated to the House, or in which its concurrence may be requested; and the Secretary shall also certify and deliver to the President of the United States all resolutions and other communications which may be directed to him by the Senate.

RULE XXIX.

PRINTING OF PAPERS, ETC.

1. Every motion to print documents, reports, and other matter transmitted by either of the Executive Departments, or to print memorials, petitions, accompanying documents, or any other paper, except bills of the Senate or House of Representatives, resolutions submitted by a Senator, communications from the legislatures or conventions, lawfully called, of the respective States, and motions to print by order of the standing or select committees of the Senate, shall, unless the Senate otherwise order, be referred to the Committee on Printing. When a motion is made to commit with instructions, it shall be in order to add thereto a motion to print.

2. Motions to print additional numbers shall also be referred to the Committee on Printing; and when the committee shall report favorably the report shall be accompanied by an estimate of the probable cost thereof; and when the cost of printing such additional numbers shall exceed the sum of five hundred dollars, the concurrence of the House of Representatives shall be necessary for an order to print the same.

3. Every bill and joint resolution introduced on leave or reported from a committee, and all bills and joint resolutions received from the House of Representatives, and all reports of committees shall be printed, unless, for the dispatch of the business of the Senate, such printing may be dispensed with.

RULE XXX.

WITHDRAWAL OF PAPERS.

1. No memorial or other paper presented to the Senate, except original treaties finally acted upon, shall be withdrawn from its files except by order of the Senate. But when an act

2 S R

may pass for the settlement of any private claim. the Secretary is authorized to transmit to the officer charged with the settlement the papers on file relating to the claim.

2. No memorial or other paper upon which an adverse report has been made shall be withdrawn from the files of the Senate unless copies thereof shall be left in the office of the Secretary.

RULE XXXI.

REFERENCE OF CLAIMS ADVERSELY REPORTED.

Whenever a committee of the Senate. to whom any claim has been referred, reports adversely. and the report is agreed to, it shall not be in order to move to take the papers from the files for the purpose of referring them at a subsequent session. unless the claimant shall present a petition therefor. stating that new evidence has been discovered since the report. and setting forth the substance of such new evidence.

RULE XXXII.

BUSINESS CONTINUED FROM SESSION TO SESSION.

At the second or any subsequent session of a Congress. the legislative business of the Senate which remained undetermined at the close of the next preceding session of that Congress shall be resumed and proceeded with in the same manner as if no adjournment of the Senate had taken place; and all papers referred to committees and not reported upon at the close of a session of Congress shall be returned to the office of the Secretary of the Senate. and be retained by him until the next succeeding session of that Congress, when they shall be returned to the several committees to which they had previously been referred.   •

RULE XXXIII.

PRIVILEGE OF THE FLOOR.

1. No person shall be admitted to the floor of the Senate while in session. except as follows:

The officers of the Senate.

Members of the House of Representatives.   The Sergeant-at-Arms, and the Clerk of the House.

The President of the United States. and his private secretary.

The heads of Departments.
Ministers of the United States.
Foreign ministers.
Ex-Presidents and ex-Vice-Presidents of the United States.
Ex-Senators and Senators-elect.
Judges of the Supreme Court.
Governors of States and Territories.
General of the Army.
Admiral of the Navy.
Members of national legislatures of foreign countries.

Private secretaries of Senators, duly appointed in writing; and the Librarian of Congress, and the Assistant Librarian in charge of the Law Library.

Hon. George Bancroft.
Judges of the Court of Claims.
The Architect of the Capitol extension.

2. No person shall be admitted to the floor as private secretary of a Senator until the Senator appointing him shall certify in writing to the Sergeant-at-Arms that he is actually employed for the performance of the duties of such secretary, and is engaged in the performance of the same.

RULE XXXIV.

REGULATION OF THE SENATE WING OF THE CAPITOL.

1. The Senate Chamber shall not be granted for any other purpose than for the use of the Senate.

2. It shall be the duty of the Committee on Rules to make all rules and regulations respecting such parts of the Capitol, its passages and galleries, including the restaurant, as are or may be set apart for the use of the Senate and its officers, to be enforced under the direction of the Presiding Officer. They shall, at the opening of each session of Congress, make such regulations respecting the reporters' gallery of the Senate as will confine its occupation to *bona fide* reporters for daily newspapers, assigning not to exceed one seat to each paper.

RULE XXXV.

SESSION WITH CLOSED DOORS.

On a motion made and seconded to close the doors of the Senate, on the discussion of any business which may, in the

opinion of a Senator, require secrecy, the Presiding Officer shall direct the galleries to be cleared; and during the discussion of such motion the doors shall remain closed.

RULE XXXVI.

EXECUTIVE SESSIONS.

1. When the President of the United States shall meet the Senate in the Senate Chamber for the consideration of Executive business, he shall have a seat on the right of the Presiding Officer. When the Senate shall be convened by the President of the United States to any other place, the Presiding Officer of the Senate and the Senators shall attend at the place appointed, with the necessary officers of the Senate.

2. When acting upon confidential or Executive business the Senate Chamber shall be cleared of all persons except the Secretary, the Chief Clerk, the Principal Legislative Clerk, the Executive Clerk, the Minute and Journal Clerk, the Sergeant-at-Arms, the Assistant Doorkeeper, and such other officers as the Presiding Officer shall think necessary; and all such officers shall be sworn to secrecy.

3. All confidential communications made by the President of the United States to the Senate shall be by the Senators and the officers of the Senate kept secret; and all treaties which may be laid before the Senate, and all remarks, votes, and proceedings thereon shall also be kept secret until the Senate shall, by their resolution, take off the injunction of secrecy.

4. Any Senator or officer of the Senate who shall disclose the secret or confidential business or proceedings of the Senate shall be liable, if a Senator, to suffer expulsion from the body; and if an officer, to dismissal from the service of the Senate, and to punishment for contempt.

RULE XXXVII.

EXECUTIVE SESSION—PROCEEDINGS ON TREATIES.

1. When a treaty shall be laid before the Senate for ratification it shall be read a first time; and no motion in respect to it shall be in order, except to refer it to a committee, or to print it, in confidence, for the use of the Senate.

When a treaty is reported from a committee with or without amendment it shall, unless the Senate unanimously otherwise

direct, lie one day for consideration; after which it may be read a second time and considered as in Committee of the Whole, when it shall be proceeded with by articles, and the amendments reported by the committee shall be first acted upon, after which other amendments may be proposed; and when through with, the proceedings had as in Committee of the Whole shall be reported to the Senate, when the question shall be, if the treaty be amended, "Will the Senate concur in the amendments made in Committee of the Whole?" And the amendments may be taken separately, or in gross, if no Senator shall object; after which new amendments may be proposed.

The decisions thus made shall be reduced to the form of a resolution of ratification, with or without amendments as the case may be; which shall be proposed on a subsequent day, unless, by unanimous consent, the Senate determine otherwise; at which stage no amendment shall be received, unless by unanimous consent.

On the final question to advise and consent to the ratification in the form agreed to, the concurrence of two-thirds of the Senators present shall be necessary to determine it in the affirmative; but all other motions and questions upon a treaty shall be decided by a majority vote, except a motion to postpone indefinitely, which shall be decided by a vote of two-thirds.

2. Treaties transmitted by the President to the Senate for ratification shall be resumed at the second or any subsequent session of the same Congress at the stage in which they were left at the final adjournment of the session at which they were transmitted; but all proceedings on treaties shall terminate with the Congress, and they shall be resumed at the commencement of the next Congress, as if no proceedings had previously been had thereon.

3. All treaties concluded with Indian tribes shall be considered and acted upon by the Senate in its open or legislative session, unless the same shall be transmitted by the President to the Senate in confidence; in which case they shall be acted upon with closed doors.

RULE XXXVIII.

EXECUTIVE SESSION—PROCEEDINGS ON NOMINATIONS.

1. When nominations shall be made by the President of the United States to the Senate, they shall, unless otherwise ordered,

be referred to appropriate committees; and the final question on every nomination shall be, "Will the Senate advise and consent to this nomination?" which question shall not be put on the same day on which the nomination is received, nor on the day on which it may be reported by a committee, unless by unanimous consent.

2. All information communicated or remarks made by a Senator when acting upon nominations, concerning the character or qualifications of the person nominated, also all votes upon any nomination, shall be kept secret. If, however, charges shall be made against a person nominated, the committee may, in its discretion, notify such nominee thereof, but the name of the person making such charges shall not be disclosed. The fact that a nomination has been made, or that it has been confirmed or rejected, shall not be regarded as a secret.

3. When a nomination is confirmed or rejected, any Senator voting in the majority may move for a reconsideration on the same day on which the vote was taken, or on either of the next two days of actual executive session of the Senate; but if a notification of the confirmation or rejection of a nomination shall have been sent to the President before the expiration of the time within which a motion to reconsider may be made, the motion to reconsider shall be accompanied by a motion to request the President to return such notification to the Senate. Any motion to reconsider the vote on a nomination may be laid on the table without prejudice to the nomination, and shall be a final disposition of such motion.

4. Nominations confirmed or rejected by the Senate shall not be returned by the Secretary to the President until the expiration of the time limited for making a motion to reconsider the same, or while a motion to reconsider is pending, unless otherwise ordered by the Senate.

5. When the Senate shall adjourn or take a recess for more than thirty days, all motions to reconsider a vote upon a nomination which has been confirmed or rejected by the Senate, which shall be pending at the time of taking such adjournment or recess, shall fall; and the Secretary shall return all such nominations to the President as confirmed or rejected by the Senate, as the case may be.

6. Nominations neither confirmed nor rejected during the session at which they are made shall not be acted upon at any succeeding session without being again made to the Senate by

the President, and if the Senate shall adjourn or take a recess for more than thirty days, all nominations pending and not finally acted upon at the time of taking such adjournment or recess shall be returned by the Secretary to the President, and shall not again be considered unless they shall again be made to the Senate by the President.

RULE XXXIX.

THE PRESIDENT FURNISHED WITH COPIES OF RECORDS OF EXECUTIVE SESSIONS.

The President of the United States shall, from time to time, be furnished with an authenticated transcript of the executive records of the Senate, but no further extract from the Executive Journal shall be furnished by the Secretary, except by special order of the Senate; and no paper, except original treaties transmitted to the Senate by the President of the United States, and finally acted upon by the Senate, shall be delivered from the office of the Secretary without an order of the Senate for that purpose.

RULE XL.

SUSPENSION AND AMENDMENT OF THE RULES.

No motion to suspend, modify, or amend any rule, or any part thereof, shall be in order, except on one day's notice in writing, specifying precisely the rule or part proposed to be suspended, modified, or amended, and the purpose thereof. Any rule may be suspended without notice by the unanimous consent of the Senate, except as otherwise provided in clause 1, Rule 12.

INDEX TO THE RULES.

A.

	Page.	Rule.	Clause
Absent himself from the service of the Senate without leave. No Senator shall	4	5	1
Absent Senators. Less than a quorum may request or compel the attendance of	4	5	3
Additional numbers of a document shall be referred to the Committee on Printing. All motions to print	17	29	2
Where the cost shall exceed five hundred dollars, the concurrence of the House of Representatives shall be necessary	17	29	2
Adjourn. A motion to, shall have precedence of all other motions	13	22	—
Adjourn to a day certain shall be second in the order of precedence of motions. A motion to	13	22	—
Admission to the floor of the Senate. Persons entitled to	18	33	—
Amendment, when proposed to any pending measure, is laid on the table, it shall not carry with it or prejudice such measure	11	17	—
When a question is pending, a motion may be made to amend	13	22	—
Amendments. When a question contains several points, a division may be called for	11	18	—
But a motion to strike out and insert shall not be divided.	11	18	—
Rejection of a motion to strike out and insert shall not prevent a motion simply to strike out	11	18	—
Nor shall the rejection of a motion to strike out prevent a motion to strike out and insert	11	18	—
In a motion to strike out and insert, the part to be stricken out and the part to be inserted shall each be regarded as a question for	11	18	—
It shall not be in order on the third reading of a bill to offer an amendment except by unanimous consent	9	15	2
Amendments to general appropriation bills. No amendment shall be received which will increase an appropriation in the bill, unless	10	16	1
No amendment adding a new item to the bill, unless to carry out existing law or treaty stipulation, shall be received	10	16	1
Amendments must be moved by direction of a committee or in pursuance of an estimate of the head of a Department	10	16	1

Page. Rule. Clause.

Amendments to general appropriation bills. All amendments
moved by direction of a committee must be referred one
day before being offered to the Committee on Appropria-
tions 10 16 2
No amendment to an amendment increasing the appropria-
tion therein shall be received.... .... 10 16 2
Amendments to river and harbor bills shall also be referred
before being offered 10 16 2
Amendments to post-road bills shall also be referred before
being offered.. 10 16 2
No amendment proposing general legislation shall be re-
ceived............... .... 10 16 3
No amendment not relevant or germane to the subject-
matter of the bill shall be received.... .... 10 16 3
An amendment to a general appropriation bill may be laid
on the table 11 16 3
No amendment to provide for a private claim shall be re-
ceived, unless.. 11 16 4
Amendments to treaties shall be determined by a majority vote.
All questions of 21 37 1
Anthony rule. Known as the .... 6 8 —
Appeals in questions of order. Every question of order decided
by the Chair shall be subject to an appeal to the Senate. 12 20 1
When an appeal is pending, any question of order or ap-
peal that may afterward arise shall be decided without
debate... 12 20 1
If an appeal be laid on the table, it shall be held as affirm-
ing the decision of the Chair 12 20 1
Appropriation bills. (See *General appropriation bills.*)
Attendance of absent Senators. The Sergeant-at-Arms may be
directed to request, and, if necessary, compel the....... 4 5 3

B.

Ballot. The chairman and members of the standing committees shall be appointed by............................... 13 24 1
A majority shall choose a chairman, and a plurality the
other members of a standing committee.................. 13 24 1
Bills and joint resolutions. Order in which the Chair shall call
for, in the morning hour................................. 5 7 1
Bills and resolutions, not objected to, to be taken up in
their order.... .... 6 8 —
To proceed to the consideration of, on the Calendar out of
regular order a privileged motion....................... 7 9 —
Whenever offered their introduction shall, if objected to,
be postponed for one day................................ 9 14 1
When presented may be postponed one day unless by unanimous consent.... .... 9 14 1
Shall have three several readings before passage, which
shall be on three different days unless by unanimous consent 9 14 2
May be read twice on the same day for reference only.... 9 14 3

Page. Rule. Clause.

Bills and joint resolutions. If not referred, they shall not be
considered as in Committee of the Whole, nor debated
if objected to, but shall go on the Calendar 9 14 4
All bills and joint resolutions reported from a committee
shall also go on the Calendar......................... 9 14 4
Before amendment shall be considered as in Committee of
the Whole 9 15 1
When ordered to a third reading they shall not be open to
amendment unless by unanimous consent 9 15 2
But may be committed before the question is put upon the
passage... 9 15 2
If committed when reported shall again go on the Calendar as bills in Committee of the Whole 10 15 2
May be accompanied by a preamble, which may be withdrawn, or laid on the table........................... 13 23
Bills. General appropriation bills. All general appropriation
bills shall be referred to the Committee on Appropria-
tions, except river and harbor....................... 10 16 1
Limitations to amendments which may be proposed to ... 10 16 1-4
Amendments proposing new items of appropriation shall
before being offered be referred..................... 10 16 2
Bills making appropriations for rivers and harbors shall be
referred to the Committee on Commerce.............. 10 16 1
No amendment proposing general legislation shall be pro-
posed to any general appropriation bill.............. 10 16 3
No amendment to provide for a private claim shall be
offered unless to carry out existing law.............. 11 16 4
Bills, private, may be referred to the Court of Claims.......... 10 15 3
Business of the morning hour, order of...................... 5 7 1
Business of the Senate continued from session to session. The
legislative 18 32

C.

Calendar of general orders. At the expiration of the morning
business, the Senate shall take up the................. 6 8,9 —
Subjects on the Calendar to be taken up in their order.... 6 8,9 —
Every bill and joint resolution reported from a committee,
and bills and joint resolutions from the House of Representatives, read twice but not referred, shall be placed on
the... 9 14 4
To proceed to the consideration of any other bill on the,
out of its order, a privileged motion.................. 7 9 —
To pass over the pending subject on the, a privileged motion .... 7 9 —
To place pending subject at the foot of the, a privileged motion .... 7 9 —
Call of the Senate. When a question is raised as to the presence
of a quorum, the Chair shall direct the roll to be called. 4 5 2
Capitol building. The Senate wing of the Capitol building, its
corridors and passages, to be under the control of the
Committee on Rules................................. 19 34 2

28

INDEX TO THE RULES.

	Page.	Rule.	Clause.
Certificates of election of Senators to be recorded in well-bound book	5	6	2
Chief Clerk, when to perform duties of the Chair	3	1	2
Claims rejected by the Senate cannot be again referred unless new evidence be presented	18	31	—
Claims adversely reported on cannot be withdrawn without leaving copies. Petitions and papers relating to private.	18	30	2
Claims, the papers may be sent to the proper officer by the Secretary. Where acts have passed for private	17	30	1
Closed doors. On the discussion of a subject which may require secrecy, the galleries shall be cleared and the doors closed.	19	35	—
Commit. After the third reading and before the passage of a bill a motion may be made to	9	15	2
When a question is pending, the order stated in which a motion may be made to	13	22	—
A motion to commit not open to amendment except to add instructions	16	26	1
Committee of the Whole. All bills and joint resolutions shall, before passage, be first considered as in	9	15	1
When a bill is recommended and again reported, it shall be again taken up as in	10	15	2
Treaties when acted upon in executive session shall be first considered as in	21	37	1
Committee on Rules, to have control of Senate wing of the Capitol building, its corridors, &c	19	34	2
Committees. Order in which the Chair shall call for reports of.	5	7	1
The standing committees, unless otherwise ordered, shall be appointed by ballot	13	24	1
A majority of votes necessary to the choice of a chairman.	13	24	1
Select committees and the residue of the standing committees may be chosen by a plurality	13	24	1
Vacancies in committees when filled shall be only to fill up the number of members	14	24	2
Enumeration of the standing committees to be appointed at the commencement of each session	14–16	25	1
A motion to refer to a standing committee shall take precedence of a motion to refer to a select committee	16	26	1
A motion to refer shall not be open to amendment, except to add instructions	16	26	1
All reports of committees shall lie one day for consideration.	16	26	2
Committees to audit and control the contingent expenses of the Senate, on printing, and on the Library shall continue and have power to act until their successors are appointed..	16	25	2
Committees of conference. Reports of committees of conference shall be always in order, except, &c., and the question of their consideration shall be immediately put *without debate*	16	27	—
Concurrent and other resolutions. Order in which the Chair shall call for, in the morning hour	5	7	1

	Page.	Rule.	Clause.

Conference. Reports of committees of conference shall always be in order, and the question of their consideration be immediately put *without debate* .... 16 27 —

Confidential communications from the President, and all treaties, proceedings, and remarks thereon, shall be kept secret. 20 37 1

Confidential business of the Senate. Penalties for disclosing the. 20 36 4

Contingent fund of the Senate shall be referred to the Committee on Contingent Expenses. All resolutions for the payment of money from the 14 25 1

Court of Claims. To refer private bills to the 10 15 3

Credentials of Senators-elect shall always be in order, and be proceeded with until disposed of by the Senate. The presentation of 5 6 1

D.

Daily sessions. Commencement of .... 4 3 —

Day certain. When a question is pending a motion may be made to postpone to a .... 13 22 —

Debate. If a Senator in speaking, or otherwise, transgress the rules, the Presiding Officer shall, or any Senator may, call him to order 12 19 2

When called to order he shall sit down, and shall not proceed without leave of the Senate 12 19 2

If leave be granted to proceed, it shall be on motion, and determined without 12 19 2

If a Senator be called to order for words spoken in debate, the exceptionable words, if required, shall be taken 12 19 3

The Presiding Officer shall name the Senator who is to speak, who, in all cases, shall be the Senator who shall first address the Chair 11 19 1

No Senator shall interrupt another without his consent, to obtain which he shall first address the Chair 11 19 1

No Senator shall speak more than twice on any one question on the same day without leave of the Senate, to be determined without debate 11 19 1

Upon the merits of the question. A motion to take up a subject shall be decided without debate 6 7 2

No Senator to speak but once, and for five minutes only, on bills and resolutions upon the Calendar not objected to. 6 8 —

Decision is announced. No Senator shall, under any circumstances, be permitted to vote after a 8 12 1

But he may, for special reasons, by unanimous consent, change or withdraw his vote after a 8 12 1

Any motion or resolution may be withdrawn, except a motion to reconsider before an amendment, ordering the yeas and nays, or before a 12 21 2

Discharge of a committee. A motion to discharge a committee from a subject shall lie one day for consideration 16 26 2

All subjects from which a committee shall be discharged shall also lie one day for consideration 16 26 2

Page. Rule. Clause.

Division of a question. If the question in debate contain several
    points, any Senator may have the same divided .... 11 18 —
A motion to strike out and insert shall not be divided .... 11 18 —
Doors to be closed. On the discussion of any business which may
    in the opinion of a Senator require secrecy, upon a motion
    made the Presiding Officer shall direct the .... 19 35 —

E.

Exceptionable words shall be taken down. If a Senator be
    called to order for words spoken in debate, the 12 19 3
Excused from voting. In calling the yeas and nays, each Sena-
    tor, when his named is called, shall answer without de-
    bate, unless for special reasons he be 8 12 1
When reasons shall be assigned for not voting, their suffi-
    ciency shall be determined without debate 8 12 2
These proceedings shall be after the roll is called, and be-
    fore the decision is announced 8 12 2
Executive business shall be decided without debate. A motion
    to proceed to consideration of .... 13 22 —
The President shall have a seat on the right of the Chair
    when he shall meet the Senate in 20 36 1
The Senate shall be cleared of all persons except the offi-
    cers in attendance (who shall be sworn to secrecy) when
    in 20 36 2
All confidential communications made by the President,
    and all treaties, and remarks, votes, and proceedings
    thereon, shall be kept secret 20 36 3
Any person who shall disclose the secret proceedings of the
    Senate shall, if a Senator, be liable to expulsion; if an
    officer, to dismissal 20 36 4
Proceedings upon treaties. (See *Treaties.*)
Proceedings upon nominations. (See *Nominations.*)
Executive record. The President shall, from time to time, be
    furnished with an authenticated transcript of the ...... 23 39 —
No further extracts shall be furnished by the Secretary
    without an order of the Senate .... 23 39 —
Executive proceedings of the Senate shall be kept in a separate
    book 4 4 2
Extra copies of documents shall be referred to the Committee
    on Printing. Motion to print 17 29 2
When the cost of additional copies shall exceed five hun-
    dred dollars the concurrence of the House shall be neces-
    sary 17 29 2
Extracts from the executive journal shall not be given without
    an order of the Senate .... 23 39 —

F.

Floor of the Senate. Persons entitled to admission on the 18 33 1

G.

	Page.	Rule.	Clause.
Galleries to be cleared and the doors closed, on discussing a question requiring secrecy. The Chair shall direct the	19	35	—
General appropriation bills. All general appropriations bills shall be referred to the Committee on Appropriations except river and harbor	10	16	1
To proceed to the consideration of, a privileged motion...	7	9	—
Amendments to. No amendment shall be received which shall increase the appropriation, unless to carry out some existing law, or resolution of the Senate, or by direction of a standing or select committee, or in pursuance of an estimate of the head of a Department	10	16	1
All amendments proposing to increase an appropriation shall one day previous to being offered be referred to the Committee on Appropriations	10	16	2
No amendment shall be proposed to an amendment increasing the amount in such amendment	10	16	2
Amendments moved by direction of a committee shall be first referred to the Committee on Appropriations	10	16	2
No amendment proposing general legislation, or that is not germane or relevant to the subject of the bill, shall be received	10	16	3
No amendment to any item or clause that does not directly relate thereto shall be received	10	16	3
All questions of relevancy of amendments shall be decided by the Senate and without debate	11·	16	3
No amendment providing for a private claim, unless to carry out a law or treaty stipulation, shall be received..	11	16	4
Any amendment to a general appropriation bill may be laid on the table	11	16	3
General legislation to general appropriation bills. No amendment shall be admitted proposing	10	16	3
General orders. (See *Calendar.*)			
Germane. No amendment to any general appropriation bill shall be offered which is not relevant or	10	16	3

I.

Impeachment, court of. Proceedings recorded	4	4	2
Indefinite postponement. When a question is pending a motion may be made for	13	22	—
Indian treaties shall, unless transmitted by the President in confidence, be acted upon in legislative session	21	37	3
Injunction of secrecy. All confidential communications from the President, and all treaties, and remarks and proceedings thereon, are embraced within the	20	36	3
All information given or remarks made by a Senator touching the character or qualifications of a nominee, and all votes on a nomination, are within the	22	38	2
A person nominated may be notified of charges made against him, but the name of the person making them shall not be disclosed	22	38	2

Page. Rule. Clause.

Injunction of secrecy. A Senator disclosing the confidential or
   secret business of the Senate shall be liable to expulsion   20   36   1
An officer of the Senate committing a like offense shall be
   dismissed and punished for contempt...................   20   36   4

J.

Journal. A quorum being present, the Journal of the previous
   day's session shall be read, and any mistake in the entries corrected..   4   3   1
The reading of the, shall not be suspended unless by unanimous consent   4   3   1
A motion to amend the Journal shall be deemed a privileged question and be proceeded with until disposed of..   4   3   1
The proceedings of the Senate shall be briefly and accurately stated on the   4   4   1
Every vote of the Senate, and a brief statement of each
   memorial or paper presented, shall be entered on the ...   4   4   1
The legislative. executive, and impeachment proceedings
   of the Senate shall be each recorded in a separate......   4   4   2

L.

Laid on the table. The preamble to a bill or resolution may,
   without carrying the bill or resolution, be..............   13   23   —
A motion to reconsider may be laid on the table without
   carrying the subject, and shall be a final disposition
   thereof   8   13   1
An amendment to a general appropriation bill may be....   11   13   3
An appeal from the decision of the Chair may be.........   12   20   1
When a question is pending a motion may be made to lay
   on the table, which shall be decided without debate....   13   22   —
Leave to introduce a bill. May be offered if no objection..   9   14   1
Leave of the Senate. A motion to reconsider shall not be with-
   drawn without......................................   12   21   2
No Senator shall absent himself from the service of the
   Senate without   4   5   1
No Senator shall speak more than twice on any one ques-
   tion on the same day without   11   19   1
A Senator when called to order shall sit down and shall not
   proceed without......................................   12   19   2
No memorial or other paper, except original treaties, shall
   be withdrawn without.........   17   30   1
Legislative business. The legislative business of the Senate shall
   be continued from session to session of the same Congress..   18   32   —
The legislative proceedings of the Senate shall be recorded
   in a separate book....................................   4   4   2

M.

	Page.	Rule.	Clause.

Majority. A motion to reconsider a vote may be decided by a — 9, 13, 1

All questions upon a treaty, except on the question of ratification, and on a motion to postpone indefinitely, shall be by a — 21, 37, 1

Memorials and petitions shall be referred without putting the question — 6, 7, 3

Before being presented or read they shall be signed, and a brief statement of their contents shall be made — 6, 7, 4

Of foreign citizens or subjects shall not be received unless through the President — 6, 7, 4

Where an adverse report has been made they shall not be withdrawn, unless copies are left with the Secretary — 18, 30, 2

Where an adverse report has been agreed to they shall not be referred from the files, unless with new evidence — 18, 31, —

Shall not be withdrawn from the files without leave of the Senate — 17, 30, 1

When an act has passed for the settlement of a private claim, the Secretary may transmit the papers to the accounting-officers — 17, 30, 1

Merits of the question proposed to be considered. It shall not be in order to discuss the — 6, 7, 2

Messages from the President and from the House of Representatives may be received at any state of the business except. — 16, 28, 1

Messages to the House and communications to the President shall be taken by the Secretary — 17, 28, 2

Morning business. Order in which it is laid before the Senate, after the Journal is read — 5, 7, 1

Until concluded, or until 1 o'clock, no motion to proceed to the consideration of any bill, resolution, &c., upon the Calendar shall be entertained unless by unanimous consent, and shall not be subject to amendment, and shall be decided without debate on the merits of the subject — 5, 7, 2

At the conclusion of the, for each day, unless otherwise ordered, the Calendar of bills and resolutions shall be proceeded with until 2 o'clock — 6, 8, —

Morning hour. The order of business, which shall not be interrupted, unless by unanimous consent, prescribed — 5, 7, 1

No motion to proceed to the consideration of subjects on the Calendar shall be received, except by unanimous consent, during the — 5, 7, 2

A motion received by unanimous consent to take up a subject shall not be open to amendment nor debate on the merits of the question — 6, 7, 2

What subjects shall be taken up during any remaining portion of the — 5, 7, 1

Motions. Before a motion shall be debated it shall, if required, be reduced to writing — 12, 21, 1

Which may be made when a question is under consideration; the order and precedence of which — 13, 22, —

3 S R

Page. Rule. Clause.

Motions. A motion or resolution may be withdrawn or modified
    before a division, amendment, or ordering of the yeas and
    nays.. 11 21 2
  A motion to reconsider shall not be withdrawn without leave
    of the Senate................................... 12 21 2
  A motion to discharge a committee shall lie over one day
    for consideration, unless by unanimous consent......... 16 26 2

N.

Nominations. The question on their confirmation shall not be
    put on the same day on which they are received, nor on
    the day on which they may be reported.............21, 22 38 1
  Discussions upon the character and qualifications of a nomi-
    nee and the votes upon a nomination shall be keep secret. 22 38 2
  The person nominated may be notified of charges against
    him, but the name of the party making them shall not be
    disclosed.. 22 38 2
  A motion to reconsider the vote on a nomination may be
    made within two days of actual session................ 22 38 3
  Notice of confirmation shall not be sent to the President
    until the expiration of two days of actual session...... 22 38 4
  When the President has been notified of a confirmation, a
    motion to reconsider must be accompanied by a request
    to the President to return the resolution of confirmation. 22 38 3
  A motion to reconsider the vote on a nomination may be
    laid on the table, which shall be final................ 22 38 3
  Upon an adjournment of Congress, or a recess of more than
    thirty days, all motions to reconsider shall fall, and the
    nominations stand as confirmed or rejected, as the case
    may be.. 22 38 5
  Not confirmed or rejected at one session shall not be con-
    sidered at the next session unless renominated.......... 22 38 6
  Upon an adjournment of Congress, or on taking a re-
    cess of thirty days, all nominations not finally acted upon
    shall be returned to the President.................... 22 38 5

O.

Oaths of office. The oaths required by the Constitution and pre-
    scribed by law shall be taken and subscribed by Senators
    in open Senate before entering upon their duties .... 3 2 —
Order of business. One hour next after the Journal is read shall
    be designated as the morning hour, during which no
    other business, except that prescribed, shall be taken up
    unless by unanimous consent........................... 5 7 2
  At the conclusion of the morning business, unless other-
    wise ordered, the calendar of bills and resolutions shall
    be proceeded with until 2 o'clock..................... 6 8 —
Order in debate. When a Senator shall be called to order, he
    shall sit down, and shall not proceed without leave of the
    Senate, which shall be determined without debate...... 12 19 2

Page. Rule. Clause.

Order in debate. No Senator shall speak to or interrupt another
    without his consent, to obtain which he shall first address
    the Chair 11   19   1
    If a Senator be called to order for words spoken in debate,
    the exceptionable words, if required, shall be taken
    down 12   19   3
    The Presiding Officer shall name the Senator who is to
    speak, who shall in all cases be the one who shall first
    address the Chair 11   19   1
    No Senator shall speak more than twice on any one ques-
    tion on the same day without leave of the Senate, to be
    determined without debate........................... 11   19   1
    A motion to take up a subject shall not be open to debate
    on the merits of the subject proposed to be considered.. 5   7   2
Order, questions of. A question of order may be raised at any
    time, and shall be decided by the Chair, *without debate*.. 12   20   1
    An appeal may be taken from the decision of the Chair on
    a question of order................................... 12   20   1
    The Chair may submit any question of order to the decis-
    ion of the Senate................................... 12   20   2
    When an appeal is taken from the decision of the Chair,
    any subsequent question of order or appeal shall be de-
    cided *without debate*............................... 12   20   1
    An appeal may be laid on the table, which shall be re-
    garded as sustaining the decision of the Chair........ 12   20   1

P.

Papers. When the reading of a paper is called for, and objec-
    tion be made, it shall be submitted to the Senate without
    debate.. 7   11   —
    No papers, except original treaties, shall, without leave of
    the Senate, be withdrawn from its files............... 17   30   1
    When an act has passed for the settlement of a private
    claim, the Secretary may transmit the papers to the
    accounting-officers.................................. 17   30   1
    When a claim has been adversely reported on, and the re-
    port be agreed to, the papers shall not be referred from
    the files without new evidence....................... 18   31   —
    Where an adverse report has been made, papers shall not be
    withdrawn without leaving copies with the Secretary.. 18   30   2
Pending measure. Amendment proposed to any, is laid on the
    table without carrying the measure to the table or preju-
    dicing the same.................................... 11   17   —
Petitions, before being presented, must be signed, and a brief
    statement of their contents made..................... 6   7   4
    Order in which the Chair shall call for, in the morning hour. 5   7   1
    No petition or other paper signed by citizens or subjects of
    a foreign power shall be received unless through the
    President 6   7   4

Petitions. Every petition shall be referred, of course. without
    putting the question, unless there be objection......... 6   7   3
Plurality of votes. Select committees and the members of stand-
    ing committees (except the chairman) shall be elected
    by a.. 13   24   1
Postpone indefinitely. When a question is pending. a motion
    may be made to.................................... 13   22   —
Preamble to a resolution. The question shall be first put upon
    the resolution and last on the preamble............. 13   23   —
    To a resolution may be withdrawn before an amendment
    or ordering of the yeas and nays. It may also be laid
    on the table.. 13   23   —
    To a bill shall be last put to question and may also be laid
    on the table.. 13   23   —
Presiding Officer of the Senate. In the absence of the Vice-Presi-
    dent. the Senate shall choose a President *pro tempore*.... 3   1   1
    In the absence of the Vice-President and pending the elec-
    tion of a President *pro tempore* the Secretary. or in his
    absence the Chief Clerk. shall perform the duties of the
    Chair... 3   1   2
    He shall have the right to name a Senator to occupy the
    chair. who shall not hold beyond an adjournment except. 3   1   3
    The Presiding Officer shall decide every question of order
    without debate. subject to an appeal to the Senate..... 12   20   1
    He may submit any question of order without decision to
    the Senate... 12   20   2
Printing. Every motion to print. except to print bills, reports
    of committees. resolutions. communications from State
    legislatures and conventions. and motions to print. made
    by direction of committees. shall be referred to the Com-
    mittee on 17   29   1
    All reports of committees. unless for the dispatch of busi-
    ness the printing be dispensed with. shall be printed... 17   29   3
    Motions to print additional numbers shall be referred to
    the Committee on 17   29   2
    When the cost of printing additional numbers shall exceed
    five hundred dollars. it shall be by concurrent resolution. 17   29   2
    Every bill, joint resolution, and report of committee shall
    be printed. unless................................... 17   29   3
Private bill. May be referred to Court of Claims............. 10   15   3
Private claim. No memorial or other paper shall be withdrawn
    from the files without leave of the Senate.............. 17   30   1
    Where a private act has passed. the Secretary may trans-
    mit the papers to the officer charged with the settlement. 17   30   1
    No private claim. which has been rejected. shall be again
    referred from the files without new evidence........... 18   31   —
    Where an adverse report has been made on a private claim.
    the papers shall not be withdrawn without leaving copies. 18   30   2
    No amendment shall be proposed to any general appropri-
    ation bill whose object is to provide for a....... 11   16   4

	Page.	Rule.	Clause.

Private secretary of Senator shall only be admitted to the floor except he is duly appointed to act as such by the Senator — 19, 33, 2

Privileged motions, save as against a motion to adjourn, to proceed to executive business, or questions of privilege, certain, are, and shall be, decided without debate — 7, 9, —

Q.

Question of order shall be decided by the Chair, without debate, subject to an appeal to the Senate. Every — 12, 20, 1

The Chair may submit any question of order to the decision of the Senate — 12, 20, 2

When an appeal is taken from the decision of the Chair, any subsequent question of order or appeal shall be decided without debate — 12, 20, 1

An appeal from the decision of the Chair may be laid on the table, which shall be held to affirm the decision of the Chair — 12, 20, 1

Questions of privilege. A motion to amend or correct the Journal shall be deemed a, and shall be proceeded with until disposed of — 4, 3, 1

When in order — 5, 6, 1

Certain privileged motions may be submitted — 7, 9, —

Question under debate contains several points, any Senator may call for a division. If the — 11, 18, —

But a motion to strike out and insert shall not be divided — 11, 18, —

Question under debate. But, pending a motion to strike out and insert, each part shall be regarded as a question; and the part to be stricken out shall be first open to amendment, 11, 18, —

Quorum. The journal of the proceedings of the preceding day shall be read, there being present a — 4, 3, 1

Shall consist of a majority of the Senators duly chosen and sworn — 4, 3, 2

The presence of a quorum being questioned, the Chair shall direct the roll to be called to ascertain the presence of a, 4, 5, 2

A majority of the Senators present may request or compel the attendance of Senators to make a — 4, 5, 3

Pending the execution of the order requiring the presence of absent Senators, no debate or motion shall be in order but to adjourn — 4, 5, 3

R.

Reading of a paper. When the reading of a paper is called for, and it be objected to, it shall be decided by the Senate without debate — 7, 11, —

Recess. Pending the consideration of a question, a motion, which shall be decided without debate, may be made for a — 13, 22, —

Recess of the Senate for more than thirty days. All nominations and motions to reconsider nominations shall fall upon a. 22, 38, 5

Page. Rule. Clause.

Reconsideration. A motion to reconsider may be made by any
  one voting on the side that prevailed................... 8   13   1
A motion to reconsider may be made within the two next
  days of actual session, and shall be decided by a majority. 8   13   1
When a bill or other matter shall have gone out of the possession of the Senate, the motion to reconsider shall be
  accompanied by a request for the return of the same..... 8   13   2
Which last motion shall be determined at once and without debate.. 8   13   2
If the Senate shall refuse to reconsider a vote, or upon consideration shall reaffirm its first decision, it shall not be
  in order to move to reconsider.......................... 8   13   1
A motion to reconsider may be laid on the table without
  prejudice to the main question......................... 8   13   1
And if laid on the table, shall be a final disposition of the
  motion 8   13   1
A motion to reconsider shall not be withdrawn without
  leave of the Senate................................... 12   21   2
A motion to reconsider a vote on a nomination may be laid
  on the table, and shall be final....................... 22   38   3
A motion to reconsider a vote on a nomination returned to
  the President must be accompanied by a request for its
  return to the Senate.................................. 22   38   3
Motions to reconsider nominations shall fall upon a recess
  of thirty days or on final adjournment 22   38   5
Reduced to writing. Before a motion shall be debated it shall, if
  required, be.. 12   21   1
Reference to a committee. A motion to refer shall not be open to
  amendment unless it be to add instructions............ 16   26   1
A motion to refer to a standing committee shall have pre-
  cedence of a motion to refer to a select committee....... 16   26   1
Every bill and joint resolution shall be read twice before. 9   14   3
Before the final vote on the passage of a bill or resolution
  it shall be in order to move its........................ 9   15   2
Relevant to the subject-matter thereof. No amendment shall be
  proposed to any general appropriation bill which shall
  not be germane or.................................... 10   16   3
Reports of committees. The order in which they shall be called
  for by the Chair in the morning hour................... 5   7   1
If objected to, the consideration of the report of a committee shall lie over one day............................. 16   26   2
All reports of committees shall be printed, unless for the
  dispatch of business the printing be dispensed with..... 17   29   3
Reports of committees of conference shall always be in order, and
  when made the question of their consideration shall be
  immediately put and decided without debate........... 16   27   —
Resolutions. The order in which they shall be called for by the
  Chair in the morning hour......... 5   7   1
Not objected to, to be taken up in their order............ 6   8   —

Page. Rule. Clause.

Resolutions. When accompanied by a preamble, the question shall be first put on the resolution, then on the preamble, which may be withdrawn or laid on the table.......... 13 23 —
A resolution may be withdrawn or modified by the mover before an amendment or ordering of the yeas and nays. 12 21 2
A resolution to pay money out of the contingent fund shall be referred to the Committee on Contingent Expenses.. 14 25 1
All resolutions shall, if their consideration be objected to, lie over one day..... .... 9 14 5
Revenue bills, to proceed to the consideration of, a privileged motion .... 7 9 —
Rules. No motion to suspend, modify, or amend any rule, except on one day's notice in writing .... 23 40 —
Any rule may be suspended without notice by unanimous consent, except .... 23 40 —
But no motion shall be in order to suspend the rule 12, in respect to voting................................. ...... 23 40 —

S.

Secrecy. The galleries shall be cleared and the doors closed on the discussion of a question that may require........... 19 35 —
All confidential communications from the President, and all treaties and debates and proceedings thereon, shall be kept secret.............. .... 20 36 3
All matters touching the character and qualifications of a nomination and all votes and proceedings thereon shall be kept secret..... .... 22 38 2
A Senator disclosing the confidential or secret business of the Senate shall be liable to expulsion 20 36 4
An officer of the Senate committing a like offense shall be dismissed and punished for a contempt................ 20 36 4
Secretary of Senate. When to perform duties of the Chair.... 3 1 2
To keep record of certificates of election of Senators..... 5 6 2
Senate Chamber. Shall not be granted for any other purpose than for the use of the Senate.......................... 19 34 1
Senators. Not to absent themselves from the service of the Senate without leave....... .... 4 5 1
Not to speak but once, and for five minutes only, on bills and resolutions on the calendar not objected to......... 6 8 —
Special orders. The unfinished business shall take precedence of the........ .... 7 10 1
Consideration of the Calendar of bills and resolutions at the conclusion of morning business until 2 o'clock takes precedence of .... 6 8 —
Any subject may be made a special order by a vote of two-thirds............. .... 7 10 1
Unless there be unfinished business, the Chair shall lay before the Senate the...... .... 7 10 1

Page. Rule. Clause.

Special orders. Special orders for the same hour and day shall
have precedence according to the time at which they
were made such   7   10   2
Special orders shall not lose their character as such unless
by a vote of the Senate   7   10   2
Dvery special order shall, unless there be unfinished business, be called up when the hour assigned shall arrive..   7   10   1
Speak more than twice in any one debate on the same day without leave of the Senate. No Senator shall..............   11   19   1
Speak. The Presiding Officer shall name who is to speak, but
the Senator first rising shall in all cases first.......... 11   19   1
Suspension of the rules. One day's notice in writing required to
suspend. amend, or modify any rule of the Senate, except. 23   40   —
Suspension of the rules. The 12th rule in relation to voting
shall never, under any circumstances, be suspended 23   40   —

T.

Table. An amendment to a general appropriation bill may be
laid on the...   11   16   3
A motion to reconsider may be laid on the................   8   13   1
And if carried shall be held to be a final disposition of the
motion   8   13   1
When an amendment proposed to any pending measure is
laid on the, it shall not carry with it, or prejudice, such
measure   11   17   —
When a question is pending a motion may be made to lay
on the, which shall be decided without debate.........   13   22   —
Preamble of a bill or resolution may be withdrawn or laid
on the, without prejudice to the bill or resolution......   13   23   —
An appeal from the decision of the Chair may be laid on
the....   12   20
If laid on the table it shall be held as affirming the decision of the Chair......................................   12   20   1
All resolutions, reports of committees, motions to discharge
a committee, and subjects from which a committee may
be discharged, shall lie over one day for consideration..   16   26   2
Treaties. When a treaty is laid before the Senate no motion
shall be made in reference to it but to refer or to print it. 20   37   1
A treaty shall not be considered on the same day that it is
reported, if objected to...........   20   37   1
After being acted upon as in Committee of the Whole it
shall be reported to the Senate.........................   21   37   1
When the question will be, if amended, on concurring in
the amendments made in Committee of the Whole......   21   37   1
After which the resolution of ratification may be proposed
on a subsequent day..................................   21   37   1
When the question shall be on the resolution of ratification
no amendment shall be in order........................   21   37   1

Page Rule. Clause.

Treaties. The question of ratification and a motion to postpone indefinitely shall each require a vote of two-thirds...... 21 37 1

All amendments and other motions may be decided by a majority...... 21 37 1

Shall be resumed at the second or any subsequent session of the same Congress, at the stage when last acted upon. 21 37 2

When proceedings shall terminate with a Congress they shall be resumed *de novo*...... 21 37 2

Indian treaties shall, unless transmitted by the President in confidence, be acted upon in legislative session...... 21 37 3

U.

Unanimous consent. The reading of the Journal may be suspended by...... 4 3 1

Until the business of the morning hour is concluded, no motion to proceed to any other subject shall be received, unless by...... 5 7 2

After a decision is announced, a Senator may change or withdraw his vote by...... 8 12 1

When the Senate shall refuse to reconsider a vote, or re-affirm its first decision, no motion to reconsider can be received, but by...... 8 13 1

Each bill shall receive three readings before passage on three different days, unless by...... 9 14 2

A bill may be read twice for reference, but not considered as in Committee of the Whole, nor debated, unless by... 9 14 3

No amendment shall be proposed to a bill on its third reading, unless by...... 9 15 2

All resolutions shall lie over one day, unless by...... 9 14 5

All resolutions, reports of committees, motions to discharge a committee, and subjects from which a committee may be discharged, shall lie over one day, unless by...... 16 26 2

No rule of the Senate can be suspended without notice, unless by, except Rule 12...... 23 40 --

Treaties shall not be acted upon on the day on which they are reported, unless by...... 20 37 1

Resolution of ratification shall not be considered on the same day it is proposed, unless by...... 21 37 1

Nominations shall not be confirmed on the day they are received, or on which reported, unless by...... 22 38 1

Order of morning business only changed by...... 5 7 1

Unfinished business, which shall be the business upon which the Senate is engaged at its adjournment, shall be laid before the Senate at the expiration of the morning hour and have preference over the special orders...... 7 10 1

Consideration of the calendar of bills and resolutions at the conclusion of the morning business, until 2 o'clock, takes precedence of...... 6 8 —

Page. Rule. Clause.

Unfinished business of a session. The legislative business of the
    Senate shall be continued from session to session of the
    same Congress 18   32   —

V.

Vacancies in committees, when filled by the Presiding Officer,
    shall, unless otherwise ordered, be only to fill up the
    number on the committee.................................... 14   24   2
Vice-President. In the absence of the Vice-President, the Sen-
    ate shall choose a President *pro tempore*................ 3   1   1
    In the absence of the, and pending the election of a Presi-
    dent *pro tempore*, the Secretary, or, in his absence, the
    Chief Clerk, shall perform the duties of the Chair...... 3   1   2
Voting. When the yeas and nays are called, each Senator shall,
    unless excused from voting, answer when his name is
    called without debate.................................... 8   12   1
    Proceedings, when a Senator shall be called on for reasons
    for declining to vote, shall be without debate.......... 8   12   2
    Further proceedings shall not be had until after the result
    is announced.. 8   12   2
    A Senator shall not be permitted to vote after the result is
    announced. 8   12   1
    But he may, for special reasons, by unanimous consent,
    withdraw or change his vote............................. 8   12   1

W.

Withdrawal of a motion or resolution. A resolution or motion
    may be withdrawn at any time before amendment or or-
    dering of the yeas and nays............................. 12   21   2
    Preamble to a resolution may be withdrawn before amend-
    ment or ordering of the yeas and nays.................. 13   23   —
    A motion to reconsider shall not be withdrawn without
    leave of the Senate.................................... 12   21   2
Withdrawal of papers. No papers except original treaties shall
    be withdrawn from the files without leave of the Senate. 17   30   1
    Where an act has passed for a private claim, the papers
    may be sent by the Secretary to the accounting officers. 17   30   1
    No petition on which an adverse report has been made shall
    be withdrawn without leaving copies.... 18   30   2
    Claims adversely reported on shall not be again referred
    without new evidence.................................. 18   31   —
Without debate. In ascertaining the presence of a quorum, the
    proceedings shall be................................... 4   5   2
    Sergeant-at-Arms may be directed to request or compel at-
    tendance of absent Senators........................... 4   5   3
    The reading a paper when objected to shall be decided.... 7   11   —
    A motion to request House of Representatives to return a
    bill shall be decided at once, and.... 8   13   2

	Page.	Rule.	Clause.
Without debate. All questions of relevancy of amendments under rule 16 shall be decided	11	16	3
A motion to permit a Senator to proceed in order shall be decided	12	19	2
A motion for leave to speak more than twice in one debate shall be decided	11	19	1
All questions of order shall be decided by the Chair	12	20	1
Subsequent questions of order and appeals shall be decided.	12	20	1
Motions to adjourn, for a recess, for executive business, and to lay on the table shall be decided	13	22	—
A motion to proceed to consideration of a conference report shall be decided	16	27	—
Each Senator when the yeas and nays are called shall, when his name is called, answer	8	12	1
Reasons for excusing a Senator from voting shall be determined	8	12	2
Words spoken in debate, if required, shall be taken down in writing. Exceptionable	12	19	3

Y.

Yeas and nays. Each Senator shall, when his name is called, answer openly and without debate	8	12	1
A Senator may be required to assign reasons for not voting, which shall be without debate	8	12	2
He shall not be called on for reasons for not voting until after the roll-call and before the result of the vote is announced	8	12	2
Other proceedings shall be after such announcement	8	12	2
A Senator shall not be permitted to vote after the result is announced	8	12	1
For special reasons, by unanimous consent, he may withdraw or change his vote	8	12	1
Any motion or resolution may be withdrawn or modified by the mover at any time before a decision, amendment, or ordering of the	12	21	2

www.ingramcontent.com/pod-product-compliance
Lightning Source LLC
Chambersburg PA
CBHW021444090426
42739CB00009B/1628